BODILY COURSE

BODILY COURSE

Deborah Gorlin

White Pine Press • Fredonia, New York

Acknowledgement is made to the following publications:
Connecticut Quarterly: Mischief Night
Greenhouse Review: Just Like Home, Graces
The Massachusetts Review: Fleshing In, Of a Feather, Slow Burial,
        Teen Angels
The New England Review: California
Poetry: Parents, In Bold Relief
Prairie Schooner: Second Nature, The Bypass
Southern Florida Review: Ground Plan
The Women's Review of Books: Like Mother

Book Design: Watershed Design

Cover Art: Magdalena Abakanowicz. *Self-portrait.* 1976. Linen, life size. Photograph by Piotr. S. Jankowski.

Printed in the United States of America

ISBN 1-877727-71-7

First Edition

Author's Acknowledgments
Thanks to those who helped me persevere: Joan Bierbaum, Susan Hill, Paul Jenkins, Leslie Lawrence, Roxie Mack, Sharon Mayberry, Karen Osborn, Nina Payne, Nancy Sherman, Faye Wolfe, Gary Young, and my colleagues at Hampshire College. I am grateful to Meredith Michaels, who allowed me to use her course title "Selves, Subjects and Souls," as a title for my poem and to Deborah Scott, who helped with the visuals.

Published by White Pine Press
10 Village Square
Fredonia, New York 14063

Contents

FLESH

MOUTH

EYES

HEAD

HEART

In memory of my parents
Alvin Seymour Gorlin (1914–1980)
Hilda Silverman Gorlin (1916–1995)

and

to Brad
to Alexandra and Nathaniel
and to JoAnn Ascoli Baumann, my sixth grade teacher

FLESH

Fleshing In

Keep coming, you humans, old customers of the earth,
an ancient traffic, identical birds frequenting all the months.

You're the basic stuff, the bread and butter of life,
bold, colorful pictures of boy and girl, cat and dog, in a child's book.

I like to repeat the syllable of your being for its simple sound.
You fog up windshields with your warm, small breaths,

you stink up the bathroom,
your sneakers loosen up the tuxedoed universe.

Picnicking blithely upon mean, high cliffs, you lay your tiny blankets,
plunk down your funky, tragic bodies, put down your paper plates
        and napkins

in the midst of ridiculous winds: poised peasants
licking your fingers, eating your salami and cheese regardless.

I find you everywhere, like gas stations or supermarkets,
open all hours, always in season, insisting upon yourselves.

I need you like some hypnosis, some recurrent suggestion of body
        and mind,
since mine remains on the surface: I begin from my skin,

a vacant patio, crust on dark ground.
My senses stand out like porches, and mind blows into everything
        but itself,

scattering leaves and dust and paper and hats all over the place.
I'd like for you to gather round a table, drinking cups of coffee,
        to talk shop.

I want to draw your vast bath and immerse my arm within the depths
     of arm,
my head within the depths of head,

until I am logged and purple with the human, been inside and out.
What do the lungs know of themselves, the latticed skeleton
     overgrown with clinging organs?

This way my hands could put on other hands like gloves,
my bone clunk against bone, pickets fenced inside pickets,

my blood warm in the loose fox stole of blood.
I could submerge myself in my solo waters,

my eyes, swimmers in their own sight, my body sunk into itself.
A mere pressure, a vague locale, I'm a wan Jane:

I want the human to come on strong, to be Italian,
to make me up with its heavy powder of flesh,

its rouge of blood, lips and tongue, its eyes like sexy blouses.
The human is a flamboyance with its ten fingers matched by ten toes,

its skin of all one color.
Most of all, essence: the cells sieve out impurity and leave us in their
     colanders.

I want to be that epitome.
Body and mind are all one heart, hard kernel of corn.

I will have a voice pressed from me like oil.
I will be all of myself.

In Bold Relief

These full independences, these bodies, are children, old and young
        persons,
who seem as complete fruits, living still lives.
They stand, free on all sides, benign authorities, calm volumes.

The skin too is a composure, concealing the scandalous, medieval
        organs,
a maintenance among the elements. Bodies are bland, accustomed
        friends.
They walk without root, shrubs of flesh,

come upon the scene, rendered whole, palpably stable, a spool
        of matter
whose curves bear the intimacies of cobblestones, little sovereign
        streets.

But it's life in them that prickles like ideas uprising, mean and fast.
Life is modern, too astringent a refreshment, a harsh abstract.
If it had parents, they came too soon.

Anonymous and dumb, the body withdraws from this skinny force.
No cream of significance can be skimmed off it,
no progress gained, integral thing.
It sits in its own lap in a patient recycling:

fleshing itself already flesh: the hands recognize the hands.
And always, it's lost in tactile echoes of others, masseurs of Narcissus,
an equal exchange of forms,
for sex is like two socks rolled up.
Language, that black crow, flies in and out of the mouth.

Now as selves embodied, we're inside a warm pie,
but then there's life again,
that new hotel, that sharp mercury, that heartless kid.

Right Livelihood

We're all said and done, our forms hardened, our anatomy
        indisputable.
We're not birds sent scattering; we don't budge,
curious, irrevocable cows in the road, deaf to honking.
Flesh, wing, sap, wave, and gust have snapped into their resolute
        places.
Like it or not, this is permanent: we're bodies.
Yet somehow, they're familiar, worn in, an ancestral land,
common nobility. They're in our blood, our roots.
None of nature hungers for the bread of its rightful body.
Bird bursts with bird, leaf is stuffed with leaf,
as if fat sandwiches of themselves.
We're all solipsists: the land thick with its own chocolate dirt,
the waters swollen full of only blue, air in the midst of its own crowd.
Gratified, inevitable bodies.

A turkey, a pumpkin, a rock suffice themselves,
their physical fact a great success, an apt fulfillment.
For instance, human bodies are loaded tubs, looking like flesh
through and through, packed to the skin from head to foot,
uniform as grapes, balls of wool, spheres,
any rich astonishing selfishness.

Inside, there's really a riotous cornucopia, a jungle impossible to
        bushwhack,
all the organs, colorful as stained glass.
These bodies worship in their own dark churches,
convert all the entering heathen, the heretic meat, the folly drink.
They mingle with their own, making little doll-like replicas.
Myth, with its satyrs and centaurs,
its promiscuous forms, is their pornography.

Bodies are bourgeois, properties kept nicely,
strict conventions of molecules.
The insects and fish are all obediences,
loyal salutes to their own strange forms.

The stars keep their distant audience.
The look-alike leaves and hairs, the similar furs, the thousand
        fleshes,
make the most acute distinctions.
Even sheep are individualists.

Pacific bodies. Life is tamed and calmed by them.
Bears and whales muffle its violence,
the earth holds its tantrums below.
A hand can do so much: constraint of such energies.

Lucky us, put in our places.
Planets set down like paperweights upon the cosmos.
Tall files of trees organize the loose sun and winds.
Oceans open up like giant pocketbooks, mother air tucks us in.

In Constraints

I relish talk about the transcendent imagination,
the Yeatsian bird highly wrought,
beautiful (but really heartless) in the trees,
Frost's business of the ovenbird, in not-so-good voice
in the teensy woods, singing regardless.
I mean, how could we live without metaphors,
those escape hatches, such necessary encroachments?
Adobe identity thins down its fat walls, quickly crumbles.
And voilá! Space inhabits us and from there on in,
it's perpetual try-on time, a crazy glue of cross references:
I'll be a bird, you be a mayonnaise jar; I'll soar, you'll spoil.
Metaphor is the stuff you need for endless marriages:
(Honey, you are not really a rat); successful therapy:
(It's okay to be a rat); and good fiction writing: (The rat *c'est moi*).

Yet, metaphors still presume forms, those recalcitrances,
traps and nets. Even the wispy have wisps.
Those lovely birds I spoke of are caught in their own motion,
the exact size of their wing span. After all, they *must* fly.
Though we exude possibilities in strings of yeses,
I think we're awfully constrained, stuck
in the muds from early on, infinite regresses:
forms contort into more or other forms, or beget them.

The body is the ultimate cast iron. Sure, it concedes with its
          softness
(small consolation), the pores like a trillion skin windows—
but there is the rib cage for the heart, that viscous cathedral,
vaunting its arterial buttresses and rafters, pathetic wonder.
The track and field of blood run their bodily course,
the cellular fence, and the silver atoms, bright beebees
stuck to the universe like kitchen magnets on the fridge.
And there is death, which is just another form

(to be sucked into the spikey grasses, the rocky seas)
but still with us within us.

Mothers and Husbands

Sometimes we had a half wit among us,
a stocky body, a good Joe. We would laugh
when she put on her girdle, Sumi wrestler style,
writhing like a fish in a net, the extra flesh rising up
like a head of beer, and we would sit superior on the bed
watching the comedy of her body, not ours. Children.
Other times she was vacuum fleshed,
the nipples screwed on tight like lids,
mass of seamless skin complete unto itself,
packed thick as earmuffs. I envied the laminectomy scar,
a former opening into mysterious areas.

I remember how at the swim club, she and I would change
in our cabana, our wet suits peeled like skin
from our flesh, damp, frothy as a cheese soufflé—
I would watch her furtively as she dressed in the darkened space,
study her like a loving scientist taken in by the subject,
her body kindly, smiling—I would one day find in my husband.

Negative Space

The mystics prattle on about its lucidity, train for its empty sport,
white sneakers perky on the courts, smile that white smile!
Pure space.
I say it is inhuman. Porcelain tile wiped clean of existence.
My children just begun in this world, all too liable.
Just watch. Soon as they emerge from the house,
it surges around them, owls swooping down for bonbons.
Vast fields beckon. Don't.
The slick streets are tracks for the invisible roller coaster.

At the bottom of the hill lies the school.
In rubber-soled sandals my children glide over the pavement,
through a promiscuous element, free passes, access.
Impossibly free, so smooth-skinned, they catch on nothing.

Bring on weather to fill space, snow up to the roof, bars of rain,
winds that will push us inside, days humid as cheesecloth.
Better my children uterine, crammed in, or caged like Hansel
        and Gretel,
the desperate witch feeds them sweets, sweeps up their
        bread crumbs.

Like Mother

Flesh of my flesh, life of my life,
you were hard to discern in the overlap.
I figured you for another bodily organ,
more ambitious and exuberant than the rest,
but still part of the same corporate bundle.
After all, how tell the difference?
You derived from primary sources, spongy genes,
biology driven like a monk copying down
chemicals from the original manuscript.
Inside our bloods matched seams.
You sipped my long straw discreetly, a socially acceptable vampire.
Your basis was so close, just beneath the skin,
short-rooted and immediate, fetal peninsula.
You lived privately, camouflaged by a huge hard hat,
a blank expression of expanding skin.

For all I knew, I was in the midst of
adding on another room, finishing some undone
pubescent details. Asleep, you were indistinguishable
from the rest of the jungle in your snug niche,
placid Tarzan hanging onto the umbilical vine
without swinging much, cargo packed securely
in a box sized to your progress, wrapped
in tissue paper to keep from rattling.
When you quickened, you were movement without agent,
a modern dance behind closed curtains.
Even now, after the brute magic of your birth,
rabbit laboriously pulled from the hat,
when you appeared, indisputably public,
declaring your sodden independence,
a blue barbarian batting space,
an island of body, skin going round and round,
I could not realize you as entirely separate—
picture slipped out of the frame, bread with its crust cut off.

MOUTH

The Mouth

The mouth tells the whole story, that psychic.
From that signatory feature issues the baby's breath,
occurs the kissy-face, concludes the ancient rattle,
all the greatest scenes of happenstance and plan.
You may view it as the hovel of unspeakable intimacies the body
        reveals,
or the cover-up, drapes of the lips pulled to, high on the head,
whatever your drug of choice.

With its escapist flaps, the mouth is the best getaway,
but it's also a crude reminder of need, of never enough,
the lips like a split nipple, lost wholeness, flat-out supplicant.
Then, it's also the sickness place, the sodden coughs
it advertises, the microorganismic hoi polloi—
and ultimately, the site for the eventual drool.
Here at the mouth is the cushioned continuum:
the skin ends, or begins, or is most skin, the delta flesh.

On good days, the mouth says proudly,
though a soft touch, I still have structure.
Like pillars, the teeth keep the porch from collapse, if not the house.
The dentist scrapes the plaque off (like death that one day will
        floss us).
I am the flesh at its best, its most sumptuous,
yet closest to consciousness, reflexive lip upon lip,
an intellectual too: a transport for words.
It doesn't get much better than this.

In Eve's Words

1.

In the garden, Eve was given little to know: the taste of her skimpy
        lips,
the tips of her fingers, the leaky excretions:
saliva issued its shallow bath.

Her nakedness was seamless, as though nature turned her wrong
        side out,
so only uniform skin showed, broken briefly by some crude detail,
a nipple or navel, rather than reveal the great genetic attic
where stacked garments, greatly patterned, lay locked in a trunk.

It was so quiet. Cro-Magnon Adam, his lips pursed, a thin line
under his beard, was anxious in paradise,
among the painted carousel creatures, stunned as horses,
(as if his subtitles could order this unaccountable green mess!)
he and the woman popped out of it.

2.

Adam bored her, and the creatures bored her,
encyclopedic life, picture upon picture, a bunch of boy's stuff.
But when the serpent spoke, he thrilled her with his scintillant
        intellect,
hissing promises in hypnotic syntax. So articulate—the way his
        undulant words
wrapped, squeezed subjects, swallowed down his length
like humping partners under a blanket. Whoa boy!
She would have it.

Hmm... Once eaten, the apple proved different. Her words were
        unlike his,
glib skin sloughed off whenever he chose, whereas hers ripened
        slowly,
mixture of vinegar and sugar, mealy, defenseless against birds,
weather, drops, and the grief of experience.
In effect, she was naked.

From her body pot, words led her, begun from the alphabet soup
simmering in cellular tureens, poured from the throat into bowls
        of sound.
Inevitable Eve.

3.

Perhaps Adam could help out, fret the act with hope.
As their bodies flushed and steamed until the coital whistle trilled,
they might glimpse something outside of suffering, some selves above,
discerned in the molecular mists, the watered ardor.
But too soon one of them would turn over.

Maybe if she pondered their difference,
his penis a cattail, a baby seal, a cuke,
how when he came, merged as they were,
he would cry out her name, "Eve!"
so she thought him "Adam."
But, no, they equalled, his tab fit.

Her flesh folded into his flesh,
they stirred a redundant batter.

Tongues and genitals carpentered to the other:

they were circular, chasing their own tail.

4.

She felt flustered by these bodies
nested inside her, only to reproduce
into a facsimile of the tree again,
as the dual boys, Cain and Abel.
With their wide branching arms
they tore like saplings from her dirt,
wrenched from the hole.
Transplants.

Foregone, she had hoped
her children would diverge from plan
travel out of this blooded wild into some Platonic state,
clouds above the bomb site. Couldn't they?
But what would that create?
Cubes and squares embedded with eyes?
Thought skimmed like cream from the brain?
Wishful thinking—it was too late.
Life sparked them into being like rubbed flint,
pumping them like a bellows, until they caught.

Seth arrived, she was old.
So she watched—as the wives of her sons,
and their successors produced the usual fare, children
prepacked in amniotic bubble wrap,
knock offs of her and Adam:
this one got her fear of birds, her thick thighs,
that one got his moodiness.

Nature manufactured each baby,

a formula framed by an image,
the two big-deal ideas of life and death.

5.

What could she do?—She could listen for God's voice,
his erstwhile walks in the garden, repeat syllables like small stones
making paths through the grasses. Inside her lay lyric ruses,
the body's soundbook that she could press and press again,
to hear its whispering liquids, whoosh of rivery blood,
the rustling lungs. She would speak of them.
Sewn inside the throat, attached to head and heart and world,
laid on its Procrustean bed, her tongue would thrust its head out
            into air, speaking,
persisting in its own language, until it spoke the language of tongues.

Art Supplies

I like them new—fresh produce brought to market,
advertising promise in their spanky packages:
the goutish aristocrats, the oils, gravy spooned on canvas;
the Victorian watercolors, oval gemstones in the box,
wet to become a delicate tea for eyes.
Elegant inks puddle silken in their bottles.
I esteem the focused pencils, blunt boys sporting flat tops.
Sharpened, shavings rising out of them like ocean foam,
they turn into dominatrixes, high-heeled, dangerous.
The pastels line up, French fries from the Mediterranean.

I'm not an artist—the truth is, should I say this?—I want to eat them.
Crisp waxy crayons snapped apart like carrot sticks,
cheesy white paste spread on salty wood sticks, cerulean malteds.
As poor pregnant women in the South eat clay to satisfy a vitamin
        deficiency,
I crave these media like pickles and ice cream,
to nourish whatever lives in me that's my own.

Slow Burial

In this conclusive place, his death would keep and contain
the rum soil soaked into him, a Christmas fruitcake.

Deodorant of cold, talc of snow, razor stars.
This is my taste in death, Puritan and chaste,
a clear, concise composition, every bit a rectitude,
slate absolute, bone done.

It's not just the bothersome rotting, really,
but that his death continues on without him even,
unending, random river. I had concepts.

I'd thought death some spikey wit, a last riposte,
tit for tat, the satisfaction of black with white,
black with white like a checkerboard.

I alternated life and death like sauna and snow,
pores wide and fat with heat, then exhiliratingly thin and
definitive with fastidious cold: luxurious extremities.

And death was some searing uprush of the real, motorcycle woollies—
at first. When he skied off the side of the earth into space,
I stood in a gaudy aberrant spring, grass coming up scarlet,
    mustard buds.

But he was buried here in Florida, in a soil of pasty limestone lace,
an uneasy land like mats floating upon the water.
I worry over him, adrift and desultory as nausea,

wallowing dopey and swamped, a soft blackening gum.
He may never die, only change form, grow and breed,
pimple and spurt as adolescence, stirred in the sexual cereal.

Queasy and anxious he must make big guesses,
he can only bend in this rubbery continuum.
Death surprised him with its sluggish unfinished electricities.

In high fruit boots, it shot him with its mud guns.

Bog People

In the gloomy afternoon, I look into their room and see them nap
the whole family in one bed. The light is left on.
Watered sleep swells them, soft and pointless,
alien to the crystal harvests of intelligence.
It would be nice to report that this sleep transformed them into
        the usual
angels or hibernal bears like bestial sweet rolls, snug under
        the stalactites.
It does not. Instead their bodies rise to the surface, pool,
look like congestive flesh. Ugly things.

As a young couple they would tangle themselves up
into a Houdini arrangement of limbs,
cry out "c'mere now, boo boo, talk baby talk."
Now multiple, hand over fist, they've produced children.
The pattern endures. Their daughter sucks her thumb hungrily,
greedy for more of herself. Their son's barnacled locale is unclear
in this thicketed bed. He steals more of the blanket. Come on, Jacob!

The body is creation's unconscious, its strange dreams:
the fringe of fingers that ends the arms,
the cauliflower heads dangling from the necks.
I see in their faces the frogs and fish, the evolutionary combos.
Now a familial clay barely dried, a slather of flesh and fluids,
their lips hang slack, breaths insinuating their nets.
Like an infection, they seep toward me, wallowing, squelched.
With my chronic cough, I go away,
where I build my stick house over water.
Who says that we ever reached land?

Teen Angels

After The Nativity *by Piero della Francesca*

The holy family gathers on a desert mountain top
above city spires. A canyon plunges below,
while French topiary trees, benign lollipops, stand in rows.
They might just as well be out of this world.

Of course this place makes no geographical sense—why should it?
A transcendent bunch lives in a transcendent landscape,
featuring eyeshadow sky, plenty radiant.
Meaty earth fares poorly, ground into floured sand.

The wisemen's coppery profiles are worn
as grave rubbings, bleached by light.
Dressed in her usual blue drapery,
Mary kneels, taxidermic, claustral,
afloat in a preternatural calm.

Only the chorus of adolescent angels, as they play their oaken lutes
know the end of the story. You sense their knowledge
behind their sullen, heavy-lidded eyes, the open caves of their
        mouths.

His lips O-shaped,
one angel sings—tries to govern the dark red office, the uvula
        visible,
hung from the palate, thin body vibrating, like a Cheese-doodle,
the eventual Jesus on the cross.

If we heard those angels sing off canvas
they would rasp like locusts and crickets,
sob clots, the donkey and the oxen, though half-painted,
braying with big teeth.

Teeth

Among the first grade set, teeth are uneasy,
first dangling from red threads, like bodies from ropes.
Deciduous canines yellow as leaves, sailboats foundered
        in the mouth.
But then, new ones come in, sprouted onions.
As if the body were appeasing
the gods in some weird ritual,
piercing itself with its own bone, to imitate eating:
mutilate yourself as you will mutilate others.
Teeth spread on a bed of gum in an intimate place—
dentists are perverts. Guys, buck or fang,
they grow higgledy piggledy, block and push, wherever they please.
Each tooth is ego and id—tame them!
Braced rows of them spell out an even type
inscribed on food, a keyboard for gastronomical music.

Short while. Because teeth are ephemeral, too, prey to insidious
        organisms,
black holes, accidents. Eroded, they break off like rock, darken like
        earth.
Older, they show their age like crenellations of a crumbling castle,
or if blessed begin their descent, gifted with mystical X-rayed looks,
Calla lilies, dervishes in white skirts, even Casper the Friendly
        Ghost.
Ended in the grave, unseen to the living, they are freed from the
        gums,
tiny tombstones, shards of the body's pottery.

EYES

Aqueous Humor

At bottom, the world is water.
Green leaves eddy and ripple on their trunks
that dissolve into muddy smudges against the sky
that meanders along the banked horizon.

Drive awhile—until you glide down rivery streets
past the stilled pools of houses, streaked with persons.
Think of phrases such as "the sun floods the room,"
or "the parade was awash with color." Her feelings "leaked."
Ask yourself the question: "why do the eyes water?"

It's hard, this exercise. The dry mind towels down the wet world,
wrings out its fluidity until forms appear, brittle in their
            distinctions.
Light flows like thermoplastics, injects to fit the specs of our retinal
            molds,
to produce precision parts that tolerate our anatomy.
Color collects like fat caught in cheesecloth,
scum floating on top of the deep soup: spectrum's rejects.
High up, we swim in lanes in our bright tank suits.

Second Nature

Their colors come upon the world, smooth impasto trowelled on,
black and white braille fantastic against the usual mundane pigments.
The cows admit the fat and plural light or they do not,
such alternations satisfy like bread and chocolates.
Their bodies create jetties of appearance
that go out onto a lake we can pet but never swim:
white is a cruel wealth, black a heavy lacquer.
Whatever hair they have looks painted,
its texture shocked by intense color—
in other words, they are total extroverts.

And sloppy flesh, beds poorly made, blowzy groined vaults
contrasted against neat New England with its geometric barns
                    and picket fences.
Shapes shift continually, slung along spines,
bellies swing back and forth like shoulder purses.
Each day their pattern changes in the pasture,
new throw of dice on the green game table.

For all their volume, they seem spun around nothing,
bundles of space, bulk of wind through the cornstalks.
They would bleed air if I stabbed them,
topple over like giant sunflowers, ring like broken bells.
Somnambulists, a sad machine runs them from far off:
they all line up, spooked and identical, to stare.

But they are so lovely. They exist as sight only,
a stimulation of the senses without meaning,
gentrified beasts from a suburban Lascaux.
Nature varnishes its surfaces like paintings.
Slick publicist, it puts on a nice face,
society dame for whom life is a favorite charity, death unfortunate.

These Holsteins are it, all the rage, just stunning things.
I enter their porches attached to air.
Deep as I could go, below color and texture, shape and mass,
I would still come upon surface after surface,
the great charisma and charm of atoms giving into an endless veneer,
a divine blather. Whatever the substance, the blocklike cows,
their plush tongues, their mud eyes, are finally fluff,
some gorgeous insincerity, their existence purely descriptive.

Mischief Night

After dinners in kitchens, the black fire follows us
inescapable to our bedrooms.
We would fan it with our breath, cold as brass.
We can't.
The clothes in the closet perspire like horses,
their sleeves deep as nostrils.
We put on old sweaters.
At our small square desks, we do our homework.
Repeat the moon is a primer, soon be wintry cold.
All the while, fashion our faces, gaudy as gourds,
listen at the window, despite our parents.
A pebble. And another, against the glass could craze.
We try to sneak by. In bathrooms our urine is cider.
Mothers come up from downstairs and listen by the door.
Not girls, those fools! Even father, guarding his athletic light,
can't recall that autumn's pull is mental.
Up the night long, in the morning,
our minds will be all over,
bright deaths discovered, pumpkins smashed in the streets.

Graces

Chilled when the dark wells
of cold rise up through their skirts
they draw their baths now
the old ladies
like Chinese monkeys
in porcelain tubs.
Hot water runs off the bone.
Their bellies puff and flush like doll cheeks.
The sun is a compact, a dusk the body matches:
bruises become amethyst.
And they are Jesuses and streaked watercolors
and the one good daughter in a swarm of jealous sisters.
Winter is their culture,
hearts twirl in the sockets,
blood mahogany and piano deep.
They claim the sheer hose worn then
is severe and lucid as any sonnet.

Near completion, they indulge
in sweets, fondle
the clitoral pearl,
persist in a prudery
of doors and drawn shades,
natural as love.
You can't botch dying.
Souls too grow up
like children. So their lives
shall run easily into death,
as a car driven soundlessly
through streets plush with snow,
will skid and circle gently
(as their fingers do, applying rouges
and creams) and allow them to go into a tree,

a garage door, a dark storefront,
whatever was no entrance before.

California

The girls ride through the nights on delicate bicycles,
their bell horns, like bracelets, tinkling of presence.

They pedal past the cool tile of the Pacific, breathe in
the fresh paint of the dark. The land is seasoned with eucalyptus.

They like identity, that scented mouthwash, genteel distance,
and its etiquette of relation: the sea will not exceed its waves,
the bird flies in its place.

The girls were born somehow. Their mothers swung open like doors,
and before them, delivered on rush mats of welcome,

were daughters, fresh news of flowers.
What a wondrous inconsequence!

Now the girls look to the common sky as origin.
Bodies smooth as teak, they toss like greens with boys

to whom they'll soon say a sisterly yes,
and put on the yoke of wicker and reeds, the sandalled marriage.

Soap and water are their ethic.
They fantasize tall, dark Italian cypresses.

By day they come to the cloisters, the vast shopping malls.
Within the rooms, mannequins stand, like Byzantine icons

in their gold and lapis blouses, their scarlet jeans.
Suspended garments calm and hold, glass cases contain.

The girls prefer this rare still air, this private catholicity.
And they'll die cheerily, assenting to the hygiene of space,

their spirits freshly squeezed
into a gratuitous juice for the sun.

Techniques of the Masters

(*After* The Annunciation, *in the* Merode
altarpiece, *1425-28, by the* Master of Flemalle)

In this painting, with their flushed cheeks,
lustrous ringlets and rosebud lips,
Mary and Gabriel could be siblings, bisque dolls upon a shelf,
darling playthings. Their drapery eddies in right angles,
a kind of platonic fabric. Dressed in a sky blue gown,
Gabriel is quite stylish, sports an ascot, as well
an embroidered tasselled sash studded with amethysts.
A band of gold beads tiny as peas holds his hair down.
Attached like a backpack, his tailored wings look clipped, ungenerous.
Mary wears a prosciutto-red gown, whose folds hang
much like a display of cold-cuts.

The duo juts out of the canvas, sculptural forms superimposed upon
     cloth,
occupants placed within a white-washed cubical.
The chamber is installed with wooden furniture
planed and sanded into geometric shapes,
a Muzak of blond oak so unlike its autistic, tragic sources.
Mary rests on the floorboard of an elegant bench made of stolid
     two-by-fours,
fretted in the back with animal carvings astride the arms.
Partly ajar the shutters show off their ingenious hinges, their precise
     jointedness.

As viewers we are meant to admire this adroit art such that industry
     produces,
the proclamation of objects, blatant constructs,
exhibitry of things holding forth in space like houses on hills.
All that magnificent confidence!

Each part dovetails the other, mortise and tenon,
fits satisfyingly like pieces snapped together, Lego bricks.
We feel the achievement of manmade artifacts executed step by step,
informed by that sober intoxicant—technique—and its happy
        narrative:
follow instructions, practice until mastery,
for life's a craft you must learn with diligence.

So why then should God be any different?
Here is Gabriel, agent of His plan, with the celestial amnio,
Jesus to be made according to specs. All's in readiness.
The Holy Spirit rides into the room on a cross resembling a T-square,
upon light beams exploited for transit.
The whole scene is an obvious set-up.

Unbeknownst to Mary, very much the scholar, Gabriel waits with
        the news,
while she pursues her study of two copies of the Old Testament,
one cradled, as a foreshadowing, swathed in her arms,
the other displayed upon the table, meant as a marvel
        of workmanship,
its bright white pages turning in the holy breeze,
its even block print registered in rows.
Beside them is a green drawstring satchel opened to reveal
a red, vascular lining.

We know what happens after this event and the next.
But in the spirit of things, let's sum up.
Those men construed Mary's mysteries
into a brief book whose four labia, like pages,
they typeset, bound and shut.

Light on the Subject

This is a breed of light I don't know at all,
not the natural kind, after the long winter,
nor painterly, the Impressionist's canvas,
dappled dilly dally, ladies strolling with parasols under the trees.
The fireworks that migrainous saints report,
that light Zen monks exchange for their heads, don't jibe with these
        special effects.
No, this light is brutal, assaults the eyes. It pours in the window like
        waves.
Militant, it camps out at night in wait and mornings
barks brightness from below. Shades snapped up
I am a mammal flushed from my burrow under public skies.

In other moods, I see an instructor who enunciates too clearly,
as if I needed a primer, or were taking a spelling test.
This is a flower. This is a table. This is another flower.
Literalists, delight: these are your (a.) likes, and (b.) dislikes.
In this painstaking light, each of us shines in a democratic lucency
that grades children and trucks and lampshades as equal phenomena.
Bleached self, I have no retreat or private darkness.

Wood Block

I often see loss in wooden things, walled rooms
where tables, ponderous dressers, and foursquare chairs
sit in state. Furniture has no sense of humor.
Unlike the swirling nests, or even the beavers' mess,
a wooden house is too upright a structure,
stiff box (Wright, not withstanding) on the landscape.

I suppose this is an old story. Look at origins.
Wooden objects fall from grace, a long way from the lives of trees,
those performers with their verbiage of leaves, ramified branches.
They exhibit such ease yet not without cost—you can see their
                twisted endurances
nailed against the insupportable sky.

We too feel made, the fallen images of the five-pointed stars,
from whom we were fashioned: our shabby bodies their cold
                clothing.
Sometimes, I think the trees look constructed, too,
their bark like siding, their branches, a cheap cabriole,
the roots installed, screwed like mollies in the dirt.

Blueberries and Cream

In this dense kiosk of August heat,
we pick them, cloistered
in their fruity hubbub. The world
becomes a single field,
a ripe berry of instance.
(Read: *Former New Jersey*
girl communes with nature.)
As we stock our baskets,
our figures are hieroglyphics
in the bushes, a large print.
I feel *read*, as if some presence finds us
absorbing upon its giant skyblue pages.
My rounded fingertips, too, feel like
the *feel* of these berries, a comparable
skin. I can roll them between
the tips like ball bearings. Organic mechanics!
Inside us, molecules bunch,
blueberries by the billions.
Further below,
configuring our basis,
the blue electrons.

But do the birds really need *all*
these berries? Doesn't nature labor
a point? The berries excite
meaning: a sensual Braille
that tizzies me into touching
until I reach truth: a wild abacus that wants counting,
a follow-the-dots that describes
some shape revealing all.
Maybe the answer sits like
these berries concealed in their baskets;
the reticulate weave blocks our full view.

Perhaps we're all of a piece, one gigundo berry,
one hyphenated leaf-person-sun-doodad-bush
glommed together behind
the separating mesh; hidden is
a unity of constituencies.

But I press the issue; I make
too much of blueberries,
a forthright fruit,
a vulnerable miracle, like the earth—
that improbable berry sprung out of nowhere,
hanging from gravity's dark branches.

Meditation on Barns

After years in New England I see its stolid barns—
those four raw walls and triangular tin skirt—
ephemeral as empty boxes, or houses of few cards.
In a certain light, they could be gigantic abstractions,
paintings on canvases by Kahn or O'Keeffe, floats rising
          into the blue,
and I get romantic,
admire their Shaker shape, ascribe to them Zen wisdom.
Curious these appearances.

Not for long—I come back to their function,
shelters installed with livestock, the cows stuporous and baroque,
the pigs nibbed for milk ink, the frizzy sheep.
The senses can scrape and hose away so much,
before they must see backsides studded with flies, dung squirted
          like Dairy Queen.

The barn serves as mimesis then:
its meat-colored walls, roof like a cleaver set into flesh.
The indoors is all the narrative we need—sausages, the birth
          of Jesus, Wilbur.
After awhile, essence and substance exchange roles:
Holsteins reduce themselves to black and white patterns,
with nose, eyes, nose, eyes, and look! a pigskin sunset.
Meantime, born outdoors, the barn stands uncertainly,
its walls splayed like a new calf.

We need both approaches to farm in this life,
the mind for the brain, children for the poems,
a place for the Adamic animals to emerge, named and hungry,
or to retreat, where form and anecdote slumber, paradisial
          and done.

HEAD

Coming to a Head

The head is a finale of flesh and muscle, surge to the finish line,
when the body sublimates its internal tissues.
Flesh was once volcanic, rushed like lava to form features,
the bubbled sockets, the blister of lips, percolated skin where steam
        still rises;
we inhabit the fossils, someone else's nest.

Features are the flesh published at last, its crescendo, all stops
        pulled out:
the nose, banked on both sides, exposing itself,
the extroverted lips, a look-out ledge, into the great hall of
        the mouth,
the original public relations team.
Look at me! my morphological Fourth of July.
I conclude here, the wedding bouquet, a fallen, soft-pointed crown.
But I can't find myself.

The Self As Word

You can hear the meaning in the sonics,
in the word itself—*Self*—the coarse Anglo Saxon,
single lisping syllable, a blunt stump,
begrudging in its sound and size and sense.

The word, however, starts out with audiophonic promise.
That long liquid "l" sound made with the tongue
tipped erotic toward the palate, Lolita-like (so far so good), flows.
But then the fricative "f" puts a stop to it.
When the lips invert, to emit that frugal "ffffff,"

of phooey, and umph, and expletive,
a disgusted breath curtails the word, stunts it.
"F" connotations include other unflattering familiars,
such as oaf, goof, thief, dwarf, and poof. A hard Germanic "k,"
a clicking finale of heels, something like "Selk," would dignify it.

Hearing the word, I think it sounds neolithic, at best medieval,
surely darksome. It has none of the abstract Latinate intellect,
nor the metaphysical swash of Sanskrit.
It could be a Neanderthal's grunt, a baby's first word
(save for the difficult "l," which would be pronounced "sef," all
          thumbs.)

But the word is mimetic: no words but in things.
A hardy kid, the self pulls the body around
like a string toy. It's not like its seeming cousins,
the skittish but ambitious spirit, the swooning soul.
It hasn't their liberties outside the body.

No, it must steep in that gloomy swamp, that sullied pond.
No house on the water here, no overlooking deck.
Blood and fluids soak through the self like a gauze,

converge at the delta. The body is everywhere.

This little word puts its finger on us for a minute,
colonized islands so hugger mugger, fighting for our independence,
elves in a world of giants, brash eyes in the potato flesh.

Selfing

Out of my way!
All day it
chants "you are a self."
Pulses within thought,
even the simplest acts,
a walk, a drink of water—
ontological torture.
Strapped to a meter
it recurs every few seconds,
a signal blinking,
a drill, or alarm bell.
Identical selves sequence
at timed intervals
down the assembly line,
products made inside a factory.
In endless supply,
the selves pass—demand
"Attend to us."
They come and keep coming.
Haunted,
I am selfed
again and again,
each one anonymous,
escalator steps in their perpetual up-down loop,
chain links circling the sprockets of a stationary bike.

Mixed Grill (or Agitated Depression)

Sludge world. Zen hell. March through mud.
Just try to open the door. Try.
Each act takes hours.
Exhaustive, as the stills that animate a cartoon sequence.
I've caught time bodily, my arms dangle, pendular as weights.
Streets slur, thick steps of black batter.
Motion is doled out, glue from rubber lips.
Truck tires hold down plastic garbage bags over manure.

Yet anxiety drums, adrenaline in a catacomb, allegro anthem.
Butterflies flutter, struggle, wings sopped by lugubrious intestines.
Electric dread.
Surf—such as tiny fishes flitting—
is contained within turf—hulking buffalos.
Inside the bank safe, coins vibrate like atoms,
flies buzz inside the giant's arms, stayed by muscle.
Viscous tumbleweed, champagne oil.
Panic mounts, like stop and go traffic,
honks its horn at that car stalled out across all three lanes.
Snowflakes fall, chit chatting, as they participate
furiously in the growing mass on the ground.

Alien

Transfused, she was rushed by space. Outside came in.
The black dome overhead—a cast iron skillet sizzling with stars—
cooked her omelette-style—what could explain this brazen
     strangeness?
Surely, it was not just local brain bubbling
but some other more malevolent agency. Sometimes
you understand the Devil, the dybbuk, crucifixes.

So this was the famous mental state
mentioned in the DSM III
come to her care of 100 Conz Street.
A black night flowed with faces, headlights, metal objects,
groundless as the whoosh of the tires sweeping asphalt.
Houses were permeable, where anything might wander in,
a bird, a truck, a messenger without a mouth.
A nightgown hung from her outline.

When the sun rose, it yellowed the world,
its transparent tape fuzzy with the lint of matter.
A pounding heart lay in a bed of flesh,
sheets askew, from the days when someone slept.
Sight paced in those eyes, a voice spoke from the throat.
In the silver mailbox, its door opened like a tongue,
was an envelope addressed to the current occupant.

I.D. Bracelets

Outside the kitchen window, even the flimsy birds
are fisted with feathers, blots on the air.
The trees are thick with their own wood.
Each leaf is painstakingly itself, oak and maple,
thousands of them, again and again on the branches.
Who can endure this filibuster of forms?
I stand by the sink, wash the lettuce, tire of its layers,
a Victorian vegetable with its petticoats and shawls.
Water runs over my hands like lace.
Lately, I am sick of identities,
creation cluttered like K-Mart.

Worse, we add our own stuff to the inborn bric-a-brac.
Hard-edged objects join the clamor:
the stainless steel top, the cast iron burners,
that faucet jutting from the sink, like a silver snout.
If I shattered these dishes, I would still have the shards.
The clown doll bounces back, the birthday candles relight.
A plunge through the glass takes you outdoors,
where space and air are.
How do you put your hand through them?

In that picture of us standing by the Toyota at Crater Lake,
your hair flowing like Jesus, mine sprung like Gracie Slick,
I see received ideas everywhere, shining from our constituted eyes.
Hippies.
Inside my school desk, my geography text was the largest
stacked under language, then history.
Culture helps out in the make-believe, the way it talks with its
          hands.
Otherwise, the self is a loincloth over a naked giant. Skimpy,
precarious, even in its own house.

Watch out for the brain with its chemical talk—
sooner or later it will falter, garble, even erase.
Vulnerable bicycle, the body's shaky theory.
Here I am the text, Deborah Faith, once spelled D-e-b-r-a,
daughter of Hilda and Alvin, granddaughter of Fanya and Jacob
Garlevetskia, wife of Brad, mother of Alexandra and Nathaniel,
Jew from New Jersey, Ashkenazi, Amherst.
Once, twice, in my life,
I was begun again, thrown back upon prehistory.
Mind was a wind, whirling inside the head
carving out canyons, electrons burning like brush fires.
Hold on, kids.

Automatic Pilot

The night of his death, I feared the body's stupid continuance,
its robotic denials. She, his wife, slept, with a sufficient heart
ruddy with blood, a shell-less mollusk washed up on the shore,
in their bedroom cool with watercolor sheets—
in short, flesh juxtaposed with the inanimate.

With a lucidity shrill as whistling teapots,
I was suddenly flushed of self,
cut from relation, the intrinsic familial intimacies.
The ancestral tree was a single stick of ice.
Beside me was yet another bleeding, breathing thing,
a concoction of life made inside its secret kitchens,
a facility called mother, a cellular peer.
My father had become a laborer dressed in the uniform of the dead.

So this was our fate—a single generation throughout time,
entities animated like children with the run of a house
in which there are no parents, nor children.

Thing of Beauty

For their annual beauty contest, the Woodabe men of Africa
preen for days. They apply pastes and liquids upon their skins
grateful for the soaking; moist pigments nourish in the desert.
They shave hairlines to heighten foreheads into sheer verticals.
This new expanse makes more space for the gelatinous surprise,
amidst the skin, of the eyes, those consolidates of light,
juicy and plump in their fitted bonnets. Piped on the lids,
kohl darkens the brown of the irises, races the whites.
The lips, blackened satins, set off the teeth to make a talking pocket.
Turbans conclude the heads in thick inverted hooves.

This luxurious process is more than vanity. They trace themselves,
the eyes outlined, the mouth colored in, skin's end or beginning,
ended or begun again. Upon every bit of facial surface,
the men dab their fingertips, sticky with cosmetics,
touch and touch their fleshiness, this intense sensuousness
by which they feel at once their own fast substances, their inborn
       masks.

HEART

Of a Feather

The birds I know, the robins and jays, sparrows and crows,
come to the skies already categorized, stayed fast in their Xeroxed
        flocks,
fenced for emphasis, coins of fixed denomination.
In a class of their own, they sit triangulate on their high horses,
        the trees,
against the easy leaves, the expansive branches.

Unlike the dogs deeply grassed, the silken cats,
the birds possess a structured softness,
shingled with clipped feathers of various lengths and layers,
just as artichokes, facets built with barbs, quill-spined.

Impossible to run your fingers through their impeccably tailored
        plumage,
lacquered wigs placed on a stand of toothpicks.
Wings, fastened compass-fashion to their sides, uplift them,
       snap shut as Japanese fans.
Raw emergences from their refinement are a rubbery cutlery,
their forked claws, pterodactyl scraps.
Deist-hearted, they tick as pocketwatches in vivid fobs.

I don't trust the romance about their free-spirits, their lyric breath,
and confess to an outrageous distaste in stating this—
that they switch on, amphetamines who sing an automatic music,
whose bolted beaks, whose stained colors denote them,
dots of an erratic pointillist's brush, impulsive scattershot
rat-tat-tatting through the innocent blue vacancies.

They peck at the dried specific grasses, the disgusting worms,
pick, pick, picking lips.
At a single glance of us, beady eyes inserted with pins,
they take semiotic flight:

formulaic shadows mean danger and nothing else
of the plural world, the friendly sorts, the curious Audubons.
We're not all cats stalking feathery snacks.

Seasonally the birds stir up flowers, scatter seeds in their poultice,
deliberate appliances whirring their blades,
intent on their own inscrutable business.
Petalled in their chrysanthemums they fail to register the lilies
         and roses.
As such they are yet another of nature's obsessions,
here are my wings again, here are my usual eggs famed for their
         fragility,
here are my brittle nests, the same points due south for winter.

In its unbroken continuance, their beings move
as endless trains of similar cars,
exact drops shaped from a dripping irreparable faucet:
we are birds that are birds, nothing but, they insist,
an empirical fact sticky as tar, stew in its own juices.

From start to finish they have no notion of our existence
nor of our reverence for them
how with the rapport of our metaphors
all of 19th-century romantic literature,
we have imagined their wings as dress for our gods,
invented them as poetry's logos, mythic mascots,
attached our aspirant spirit to their flitting movements.
And they never will know,
our calls muffled by their minuscule padded cells,
busy telephone signals, our questions sponged off Formica counters.

Look at them clearly then, as jealously guarded keepsakes,
inviolate lockets with pictures laminated

inside them of more of their kind,
mama bird, papa bird, baby bird,
capsules of identical genetic powders, a rhetorical alphabet,
bird within bird like trouble dolls, in the endless somersault
       of ongoing species.
In a causal dread, a bird is the reason for a bird,
isn't that obvious, they say condescendingly,
we are a logical consequence, dominoes' dominoes.
As delicate as they are, I can't break
the iron link in generation's interminable chain,
wedge myself in.
They sing as they sing.

Emmie and Child

(After the painting by Mary Cassatt)

In this portrait
the bold chintz
dress the mother wears
has immense influence.
It takes up
half the canvas,
a horse of fabric
like some soldierly monument.
Ambiguous roses
are strewn upon its vast surface,
a pattern at once ugly and gorgeous;
these roses, construed as vascular cheer,
or blotted lipstick kisses,
as easily suggest disease,
mysterious viruses that bring
blotches and boils, scarlet fevers, bruise marks.
But here comes the cosmos, too,
swirling its hot red nebulae,
or is that only
a horde of local fires,
mundane birthmarks
with public pigments?
From all these brushstrokes,
Cassatt produces a dress
whose dyes run in the wash.
Blues and reds bleed to create wine hues
that tinge the baby's white undershirt,
even his face and hands.
Where does this dress cease?
Upon his mother's lap, the sleepy baby,

stained at the onset
by this perfect mess,
dangles unfinished legs
into passages of roiling cloth,
flux of milk and dusk and something else.

A Set of Dentures, a Smokestack, a Knoll

Outdoors in August, laboring all day in his garden, he's shirtless,
this old guy, acting as nature's geisha, white cummerbund truss
around his chest to hold his organs in, like an obi, but more,
a head of beer, frothy sweat dribbling down the mug's sides.
He has an inoperable abdominal hernia (or, so he says)
which looks like a forsaken breast,
a pregnancy due east or west, depending on his standing.

Yet this wit, at his expense, tells us nothing of its substance.
We instantly assume this phenomenon is aberrant,
an aesthetic insult or worse, some medical drama, such as a failed
                escape of flesh,
a mad dough doubling like a monster in a horror flick
to be caught and cut back, punched down again—call the surgeons!
Never has it occurred to us that we might grow toward it,
as a kind of sun, slowly sucked into its compact hardiness,
shrinking ourselves to a shrimp's size to fit;
or considered this potential reversal of dominance—
that our goofy bodies could be its overgrown kapok.
Nature was the original bogeyman and now she's old hat:
freakishness is only what we haven't gotten used to.

One day I'll ask this man to overcome his modesty, his curious dress
and show me his growth, like a set of dentures, a smokestack, a knoll.
In turn I will lift up my blouse or pull down my pants
and we'll have a good laugh over our bodies,
which were born with nothing we cannot bear.

Common Ground

Those old darkened bricks do not strive,
these monks of earth, kernels of Indian corn,
stacked line upon line in unvarying pattern.
They take their part in this settled building on the street.
Something resides in me like them,
a worn, but wise heart, an acceptance beyond
my nervous making, whose snug, high walls
provide a closure I can take comfort in when I choose.

The bricks tell me they've been burned before,
touched by every weather. For now they author
structures above the ground, but know full well
their work will not endure for long,
being made, like us, of clay and fire.

The End of Summer

Before this hiatus, the summer was assiduous and distant.
The light did not let up, drove the poor, toiling chlorophyll.
The grass was a terse careerist.
Now in late August, the weather is close, our skins porous.
Bushes, ivied walls and high hedges huddle around us.
Plants fur over like small mammals:
the rabbit's foot clover, the nodding thistle, the velvet sumac.
Its work finished, growth doodles and rambles,
disheveled leaves slump on the branches.
Long and loose, the grass, at last, is gracious,
strewn with Queen Anne's lace, golden rod—elaborate Victorian
        flora.

We're due for a shift. I dread the dry diaspora of fall air,
bracing as vodka, autumn with its brilliant analyses,
schoolchildren who, as they file into classes, to their freshly varnished
        desks,
take their seats like jockeys mounted on horses.

Parents

Their bodies change, sudden weathers.
They come indoors like children.
Tiny chariots of hearts pull them about.
Their lives are their bodies, located there,
obvious and reduced, so in motion, they move;
in pain, they hurt.

Unanimous, unnamed energy acts around me, however,
and I respond, a buoyant justice, suspended and attained,
a body coming alone to its own occasion,
a boor of health

who wants them epitomized,
but they are too delicate and vague a stuff
for such violence of love,
for such black cheerleading.

Their dying is a disappointing
they can tell me very little of.
They smile like smoke, they yellow.
Their flesh is Kansas, looks slept on.
I do not like their bright clothes.

They will die on a day
and it shall be nothing much
an opera of small animals
a spilled beautiful glass of water.

The Bypass

Packed closely around those tuberous roots,
organs strung in bunches inside her body,
her flesh is a soil fast filling up the holes,
surgery's lavish revelations covered over.
At those former sites of such dangerous exuberances,
they sawed through bone to a heart they pulled out raw as an infant,
then grafted on the wormy veins dug from groin and legs.
A month later, the only obvious traces of the procedure are scars,
deniers of any such unruliness.
The skin is Apollonian in restraint, a dull craft.
Trauma is rarely conspicuous.
After this ordeal she looks insultingly the same,
a bit thinner, yet recognizable, with little to show
save marks hidden and fading under clothes, a dramatic tale
consigned to anaesthesia, more pills, more worry.
Sickness is a miniaturist, its crises played out in the cellular stadiums;
atomic in force, a heart attack is mere inches long.

Vital denial conspires to domesticate that awful wonder.
If she were to see her actual heart outside her,
beating, singular, impersonal,
it would seem cartoon-like, a red bullfrog.
In her silk kimono, in her spotless useless kitchen,
she could never believe it of herself.
Impossible that the heavy weight of experience
rests upon this obscene peanut,
the mind mere newsprint in the blood.
Her self occupies an immaculate residence,
sealed off from the elements, shades drawn,
set down incongruously in the bodily tropics.
For instance, fresh from the surgery, she inquired,
"Where is my checkbook? I must pay the phone bill."
"Did Aunt Miriam call yet?" Or pronounce:

"That dress is darling, dear, but don't you think
it's time for a haircut?" Lucky lady.
I would watch, mesmerized, the monitor above her head
write the rhythms of her heartbeat in a script that looked Arabic.

Car Pool

We are contained by these faithless pilgrims, the mobile
but inanimate cars, each in its stagnant pool of hard-edged metal,
unmoved movers. Putative daddies of liberty,
in fact, only a cold and singular key ignites them,
vehicular stases, prudes of movement,
fixed in their tires as teeth in gums.
All they do is roll on wheels yoked to an axle,
which limits them to pivots left or right,
the most austere progress forward and back.
Nothing on them responds to wind.
Animals, by contrast, percolate with a shivery energy,
but in cars, it is a stilled bondage,
a brute nominative housed in an engine block,
whose pistons, bound like Oriental feet,
pump in closed chambers,
the geraniums of explosions stunned by frosted valves.
And what sick music is expressed: a single note
knowing only loudness, as speed is accomplished,
a ruled sound band. I watch cars proceed in endless waves,
in a dutiful continuance, chains around the earth.
They skim asphalt, repel the assorted weathers,
never change from their exposure but rust a lot.
Fast with people in them, cars are pure denial.

Gradual Incarnation

Pulled like hardening taffy, stubbornly extruded,
this dollop of baby is still an idea in a blanket,
spun like cotton candy, on a core of air.
Her skin is a slurry still drying on its rack of bones.
Except for precise fingers and toes
she is featureless—I watch the cloudy head for shapes,
for progress of a face—the blank eyes under puffy lids,
the smudge of mouth. I try and pin her down,
swaddle her in a blanket as the nurses taught.
But she sifts through me like flour.

I might as well be a farmer nurturing the sky.
All day I drive to her in a car with tires of flowers.
Her scent maddens, impossible to place.
I circle lovingly, a phantom she-wolf suckled by sweet air.

Ground Plan

Wonderful if at our deaths some savior neatly clipped our souls,
perforated coupons redeemable upon receipt;
or some scientist split cells like hairs, sorting spirit from flesh,
one in the incoming, the other in the outgoing files.

But really! these distinctions seem spurious in the face of it.
The dirt diets on us, the leading high protein food
that peps up the mashed grasses, the grumpy trees.
Who are we kidding? Those eau de souls are overpowered by
        a stronger odor.

Yet somehow I still want to celebrate this brief life here,
cherish my happenstance, my precious little—
this caffeine buzz, snap crackle pop, chihuahua yip-yap.
I make new friends among the sparkling living things,
I mingle more, say yo, hello, to my fibrous cousins,
the foodstuffs and flowers, since we share a similar shelf life.
I feel kin to falling snow, dirty hankies on which whole plots hinge,
dustballs tanning in the tropics.

I'm glad each year for my neatly braided genes.
Now I easily greet the streets paisley with people,
the recurring filigree of arms and legs and faces,
elaborately wrought. I'm not afraid of losing myself.
Look at those claustral medieval tapestries,
where even the queens and unicorns lose their hierarchical edge,
mixed with mardi-gras monkeys and fleur-de-lis,
made from the same tragical textures,
figures woven into ground.

Taking Care

When I took care of you, I grew as swans,
pushing off banks into water,
one after the other after the other,
and hung as grapes, those huddles of feeling,
all similar with love.
Your wondrous body filled with the sweetness
of eyes within eyes, the sweetness of hands within hands.
Within your body was the body again,
my poor sick man, how much you gave me.
I warmed as arms warm in thick sweaters.
I gathered ground and sky around me
until I spun on my own, whole as a globe.
Patience poured its thick cream.
I kissed you in fits, thousands of them,
pecking like pigeons. And when I thought of
going home, it seemed a vast interruption.

Women and Dog

In Bonnard's miniature oil painting, 16 x 12 inches,
two women in a garden aid a golden-haired retriever,
whose great satin head like a furry ballet slipper with floppy ears,
summons the lust of tenderness.
One stoops to extricate a burr from the dog's paw,
or disentangle him from the bush,
as the other, her arm on her friend's
shoulder, looks gently upon the scene.

With their bud-shaped faces, lush hair,
the two resemble the surrounding foliage,
while the flowers, in sympathy, especially
the sloppily rendered mums, look doggish—
the fluffy kittens, bunnies, guinea pigs children beg to hold.
"Affection is more important than ideas," declared George Eliot,
that most cerebral author, who had no children.

One of the two women wears an exhilirating dress
like a scythe that cuts through the thicket of living beings,
crowded on this small canvas.
A classic blue and white check,
full triangular sail, it asserts
its crisp limits, a refreshing fence—Hey,
on second view, maybe she is not helping the dog at all,
but bending down to pick flowers.
The dog, then, is an irritant, leaping onto her lap, interrupting her
          pleasure.
She wants no part of it. He slides off her
sharply angled dress, stunned by its electricity.

Uh oh. The painting's ambiguous, not all blue or white.
Maybe the checkered pattern is a lattice on
which nature grows, a support—like a parent? a lover?

Maybe it has nothing to do with living beings,
an abstract network of color.
What would Freud make of the dress?
Work and love.
I say, it's a great looking dress. You should invest in clothes
you can go anywhere in, that make you feel good.

Just Like Home

The loss of self should be dark horses
deep in their feedbags, an assured and mysterious nourishing,
smooth in the heart as leathers and fur,
soft moccasins, the noses of dogs.
It might learn too the insouciance of teas and coffees
drunk down and gone, the graciousness of cakes and muffins.

Then comfort could saint us: mothers cut the red meat
fear into small pieces, put us at our ease and make us read,
that animal absorption, or play a long time as a canoe taken down the
        river.

Surely enjoyable! The self, if cajoled and soothed,
should sink into God as a cushion, warm descendence
into that light nap of Being, the Great Relaxing,
to become a nostalgia, some sepia photograph of God's,
who is not an extremity of black or white light
but usual as the sparrows and wrens persevering through the seasons.

ABOUT THE AUTHOR

Deborah Gorlin was born in Newark, New Jersey in 1951. She graduated from Rutgers University in 1973. As an MFA student at the University of California at Irvine from 1974 to 1976, she worked in the California Poets-in-the-Schools program and was awarded Squaw Valley Writing Conference scholarships. At both Rutgers and UC/Irvine, she received the American Academy of Poets college prize.

Many of her poems have appeared in national periodicals, including *Poetry, Prairie Schooner, New England Review, The Massachusetts Review,* and *The Women's Review of Books.* At present, she is at work writing a memoir about her family and starting her second book of poems.

She has worked as a public relations director and publications editor for an art museum, as an editor and writer for a college alumni magazine, and as a freelance feature and copywriter. Currently co-director of the Writing Center at Hampshire College in Amherst, MA , she serves as a writing counselor and teacher.

A longtime resident of the Pioneer Valley, she lives in Amherst with her husband, Brad Crenshaw, a poet, critic, and neuropsychologist, and their two children, Alexandra and Nathaniel.

THE WHITE PINE PRESS POETRY PRIZE

The White Pine Press Poetry Prize, established in 1995, offers a cash award of $500 plus publication of the winning manuscript. Manuscripts are accepted between July 15 and October 15 each year. The winning manuscript, which is selected by a poet of national stature, is announced the following summer, with publication following in the spring. Please write for additional details.

1995   *Zoo & Cathedral* by Nancy Johnson
         Selected by David St. John

1996   *Bodily Course* by Deborah Gorlin
         Selected by Mekeel McBride

AMERICAN POETRY FROM WHITE PINE PRESS

Treehouse: New & Selected Poems
William Kloefkorn
ISBN 1-877727-65-2   240 pages $15.00 paper

Certainty
David Romtvedt
ISBN 1-877727-59-8   96 pages $12.00 paper

Destination Zero
Sam Hamill
ISBN 1-877727-53-9 $15.00 paper

Leaving Egypt
Gene Zeiger
ISBN 1-877727-50-4   96 pages $12.00 paper

Clans of Many Nations
Peter Blue Cloud
ISBN 1-877727-47-4   176 paghes $14.00 paper

Heartbeat Geography
John Brandi
ISBN 1-877727-40-7   256 pages $15.00 paper

Watch Fire
Christopher Merrill
ISBN 1-877727-43-1   192 pages $14.00 paper

Between Two Rivers
Maurice Kenny
ISBN 0-934834-73-7   168 pages $12.00 paper

Tekonwatonti: Molly Brant
Maurice Kenny
ISBN 1-877727-20-2   209 pages $12.00 paper

Drinking the Tin Cup Dry
William Kloefkorn
ISBN 0-934834-94-6   87 pages $8.00 paper

Jumping Out of Bed
Robert Bly
ISBN 0-934834-08-3   48 pages $7.00 paper

Poetry: Ecology of the Soul
Joel Oppenheimer
ISBN 0-934834-36-9   114 pages $7.50 paper

Why Not
Joel Oppenheimer
ISBN 0-934834-32-6   46 pages $7.00 paper

Two Citizens
James Wright
ISBN 0-934834-22-9   48 pages $8.00 paper

ESSAYS ABOUT POETRY

Where the Angels Come Toward Us
David St. John
ISBN 1-877727-46-6   256 pages $15.00 paper

POETRY IN TRANSLATION FROM WHITE PINE PRESS

Starry Night
Marjorie Agosím
ISBN 1-877727-66-0   96 pages $12.00 paper

The Four Questions of Melancholy
Poems by Tomaz Salamun
ISBN 1-877727-57-1   224 pages $15.00 paper

These Are Not Sweet Girls
An Anthology of Poetry by Latin American Women
ISBN 1-877727-38-5   368 pages $17.00 paper

Anxious Moments
Prose Poems by Ales Debeljak
ISBN 1-877727-35-0   78 pages $12.00 paper

A Gabriela Mistral Reader
ISBN 1-877727-18-0   277 pages $13.00 paper

Alfonsina Storni: Selected Poems
ISBN 0-934834-16-4   72 pages $8.00 paper

Circles of Madness: Mothers of the Plaza de Mayo
Marjorie Agosín
ISBN 1-877727-17-2   128 pages $13.00 paper

Sargasso
Marjorie Agosín
ISBN 1-877727-27-X   92 pages $12.00 paper

Maremoto/Seaquake
Pablo Neruda
ISBN 1-877727-32-6   64 pages $9.00 paper

The Stones of Chile
Pablo Neruda
ISBN 0-934834-01-6   98 pages $10.00 paper

Vertical Poetry: Recent Poems by Roberto Juarroz
ISBN 1-877727-08-3   118 pages $11.00 paper

Light and Shadows
Juan Ramon Jimenez
ISBN 0-934834-72-5   70 pages $9.00

Elemental Poems
Tommy Olofsson
ISBN 1-877727-13-X   136 pages $12.00 paper

Four Swedish Poets: Strom, Espmark, Transtromer, Sjogren
ISBN 0-934834-97-0   140 pagers $10.00 paper

Night Open
Rolf Jacobsen
ISBN 1-877727-33-4   221 pages $15.00 paper

Selected Poems of Olav Hauge
ISBN 1-877727-03-2   92 pages $9.00 paper

Tangled Hair
Love Poems of Yosano Akiko
ISBN 0-934834-05-9   48 pages $7.50

A Drifting Boat
An Anthology of Chinese Zen Poetry
ISBN 1-877727-37-7   200 pages $15.00 paper

Between the Floating Mist
Poems of Ryokan
ISBN 1-877800-01-5   88 pages $12.00 paper

WHITE PINE PRESS

White Pine Press is a non-profit publishing house dedicated to enriching literary heritage; promoting cultural awareness, understanding, and respect; and, through literature, addressing social and human rights issues. This mission is accomplished by discovering, producing, and marketing to a diverse circle of readers exceptional works of poetry, fiction, non-fiction, and literature in translation from around the world. Through White Pine Press, authors' voices reach out across cultural, ethnic, and gender boundaries to educate and to entertain.

To insure that these voices are heard as widely as possible, White Pine Press arranges author reading tours and speaking engagements at various colleges, universities, organizations, and bookstores throughout the country. White Pine Press works with colleges and public schools to enrich curricula and promotes discussion in the media. Through these efforts, literature extends beyond the books to make a difference in a rapidly changing world.

As a non-profit organization, White Pine Press depends on support from individuals, foundations, and government agencies to bring you this literature that matters — work that might not be published by profit-driven publishing houses. Our grateful thanks to all the individuals who support this effort and to the following foundations and government agencies: Amter Foundation, Ford Foundation, Korean Culture and Arts Foundation, Lannan Foundation, Lila Wallace-Reader's Digest Fund, Margaret L. Wendt Foundation, Mellon Foundation, National Endowment for the Arts, New York State Council on the Arts, Trubar Foundation, Witter Bynner Foundation, and the Slovenian Ministry of Culture.

Please support White Pine Press' efforts to present voices that promote cultural awareness and increase understanding and respect among diverse populations of the world. Tax-deductible donations can be made to:

White Pine Press
10 Village Square • Fredonia, NY 14063